YOU

WERE

NEVER

ABSENT

GABRIEL GARCIA

Published by Still Grove Press
www.livefullypresent.com

ISBN: 979-8-9988793-0-2
First edition.
Printed in the United States of America.

Cover and interior design by Gabriel Garcia

DEDICATIONS

FOR YOU.

Not the "you" trying to become something.

But the one that's always been whole,

always been here, always been enough.

PROLOGUE

There comes a moment when
the seeking begins to soften.

Not because you've found all the answers,
but because something in you remembers that
you are not a question to be solved.

You start to notice the quiet between thoughts.
The stillness beneath effort.
The aliveness in what once felt empty.

And slowly, the chase to become someone
dissolves into the simplicity of being.
No finish line. No title.
Just this—
the breath, the ground, the awareness
that's always been here.

Presence isn't something you achieve.
It's what remains when the noise settles.

This book is not here to teach you something new.
It's here to help you remember what never left.

Each page is a pause.
A mirror.
A quiet invitation back to what is
already whole within you.

There is no destination ahead—
only this moment, always unfolding, always complete in
itself.

So read slowly.
Let the words breathe.
And more importantly—
let them fall away.

What matters most is not what you understand,
but what you begin to feel again:

That you were never lost.
Never behind.
Never separate from the truth you seek.

This Moment Is Not the Beginning of Something New.

It Is the Return to What Never Left.

CHAPTER 1

REMEMBERING

THE

NOW

Right Here, Right Now

Life is not happening yesterday.
It is not happening tomorrow.
It's always here and now.
In this breath, in this moment.

But the mind rarely lives here.
It either pulls us into memory,
or pushes us toward imagined futures.
It distracts us from the only
place life ever unfolds.
This very moment.

Right now, beneath all thought,
something is quietly present.
The sound in the room.
The rhythm of your breath.
The weight of your body.

You don't have to reach for it.
You're already within it.
Nothing needs to be added.
Nothing needs to change.

This is it.

The Mind's Chase

The mind is always on the move.
It races to the next task,
the next goal,
the next version of a better you.

It whispers,
"You're not there yet."

So you chase.
Achievement.
Success.
Control.
Peace.

Yet the chase never ends.

Each time you arrive,
the mind has already moved on.

It feeds the misconception
that happiness lives somewhere else.

But peace isn't ahead of you.
It's here—beneath the chase.

When the mind quiets,
you arrive.

The Habit of Missing Life

Life is always offering itself—

in the chirping of birds,

the rustle of leaves,

the pause between words.

Still, the mind is elsewhere.

Planning.

Remembering.

Anticipating.

We rush from one moment to the next,

rarely arriving in the one we're in.

Presence doesn't ask for more.

It asks to be noticed.

When you slow down enough to feel it,

even the ordinary becomes sacred.

Not because it changes—

but because you finally see it.

Be Still.

Life Is Already Here.

Noticing What's Already Here

We search for presence
as if it's hidden.

But it's not lost,
we're just distracted.

Awareness doesn't arrive.
It's what remains
when everything else settles.

It's in the stillness between thoughts.
In the space before the next breath.

You don't have to earn it.
You don't have to chase it.

Just notice.

What you're looking for
has always been here.

The Depth in the Ordinary

We wait for something profound—
a sign, a breakthrough,
a moment that changes everything.

And yet, life is whispering all the time.

In the way sunlight moves across the floor.
In the steam rising from a warm cup.
In the silence between songs.

Presence is not loud.
It lives in what we overlook.

When we slow down,
even the smallest moment
becomes a doorway.

The sacred is not hidden.
It's simply unnoticed.

The Concept of Time

The past is a memory.

The future is imagination.

Neither exists right now.

Time lives in the mind—

measured, divided, and chased.

But life doesn't move in minutes.

It moves in moments.

Close your eyes.

Feel your breath.

Listen without naming.

Where is time in this?

Presence is timeless.

And you are here.

Now is not a point on a timeline—

it's what remains when time falls away.

Now Has No Edges

This moment doesn't begin

when you notice it,

and it doesn't end

when you move on.

It has no edges,

no entrance,

no exit.

It's not a point in time.

It's the open field

that time passes through.

And when the mind gets quiet,

you realize—

you were never outside of it.

The End of the Search

What if there's nothing missing?
Nothing to fix, improve, or become?

What if peace isn't in the next moment,
but in this one,
when the search finally stops?

The mind searches.
Awareness waits.

You don't find presence
by chasing it.

You find it
by no longer leaving.

Stillness isn't something you reach—
it's what's left when you stop.

There Is no Next Moment.

Only This One.

CHAPTER 2

THE NEED

TO

CONTROL

The Fear of Uncertainty

The mind fears uncertainty.
So it grasps for control.

It plans, predicts, protects—
trying to shape life
into something safe.

But life doesn't obey our plans.
It moves in ways
we can't predict or hold.

And the tighter we grip,
the more we suffer.

Control feels like safety.
and yet, it's resistance.

Peace doesn't come from holding on.
It comes from letting life be what it is.

When Life Doesn't Go as Planned

You make a plan.

You set a course.

And then—life shifts.

The job falls through.

The relationship ends.

The path changes.

It can feel like failure.

Like something went wrong.

But what if it didn't?

Life rarely unfolds
the way we imagined.

Yet somehow,
it still carries us.

Sometimes what feels like a detour
is how grace arrives.

Softening the Grip

We hold tightly—
to outcomes, ideas,
and the way we think life should go.

Tightness feels like control,
but it doesn't bring peace
It brings tension.

Control is effort.
Softening is trust.

You don't need to let go all at once.
Just loosen.

Even the smallest release
makes space for life to move.

What you're holding
might be holding you back.

The Fear Beneath Control

We don't cling because we're selfish.
We cling because we're scared.

Scared of losing what we love.
Scared of not knowing what comes next.
Scared of falling apart.

Control is the armor.
Fear is what it protects.

Still, fear softens
when it's seen.
When it's felt.
When it's allowed.

You don't need to fix it.
You just need to stop resisting it.

Even fear can pass through you
when you stop holding it in place.

It's Okay To Not Know.

Life Will Meet You There.

Life Doesn't Need Your Control

Your breath moves without effort.
Your heart beats without instruction.

The sun rises.
The tide returns.
The seasons change.

All without your control.

Life is already happening.
Already flowing.
Already aware of how to move.

Control doesn't make you safe—
it makes you tense.

You were never meant to carry it all.
You were meant to trust the rhythm.

Flowing With What Is

Not everything goes the way you hoped.
Not every moment feels easy.

But peace isn't found in perfect conditions—
it's found in presence.

To flow doesn't mean to agree.
It means to stop fighting what's already here.

Some things you'll change.
Some things you'll accept.

But resistance adds weight
to everything you touch.

When you stop pushing against life,
you find yourself moving with it.

The Unexpected as a Teacher

Not everything that interrupts your path
is here to harm you.

Some changes unsettle you
only to reveal something deeper.

Life doesn't just teach
through clarity and ease.
It also teaches
through disruption and redirection.

The mind may resist.
But the heart can learn
to stay open.

Even the unplanned
can carry you home.

Real Freedom

We think freedom means
being in control.

Calling the shots.
Planning every outcome.
Never being surprised.

But that kind of freedom
is fragile.

Real freedom isn't about controlling life.
It's about no longer needing to.

It's the quiet strength
that rises when you stop forcing.

It's the peace
that doesn't depend on circumstances.

Real freedom is trusting life enough
to be fully here.

Life Is Already Moving.

You Don't Have To Push.

CHAPTER 3

THE CLARITY

OF

SLOWING DOWN

Life Isn't Rushing

We say life moves too fast.
Yet life isn't rushing.
We are.

We rush through mornings,
through conversations,
through entire seasons of our lives.

We measure our worth by
how much we get done.
We confuse movement with meaning.

But in all that speed,
we miss what's real.

Slowing down isn't falling behind—
it's coming home.

Nothing is missing
when you're fully here.

The Pace of Presence

Presence has its own rhythm.

It doesn't rush.

It doesn't push.

It doesn't chase.

It moves slowly,

like breath,

like nature,

like truth.

When you slow down,

you begin to match that pace.

Not because you're doing less—

but because you're finally here

for what you're doing.

Peace isn't far away.

It's just moving more slowly than you.

Returning to Your Senses

The mind lives in time.
The body lives in now.

When you return to the senses,
you return to presence.

The feel of your feet on the ground.
The sound of wind through trees.
The warmth of water on your skin.

These aren't just sensations—
they're anchors.
Each one a doorway
into what's real.

You don't have to silence the mind.
Just shift your attention
to what's already happening.

The body never left the moment.
Only your awareness did.

You Meet Life

In the Pace You Are Willing To Feel.

Simplicity is Sacred

The mind craves complexity.
It believes depth must be layered,
and truth must be hard to find.

And yet, real depth is simple.
Real clarity is quiet.

The more present you become,
the more beauty you see
in the most ordinary things.

A breath.
A leaf.
A shared moment of silence.

There's nothing missing.
Nothing to chase.

Simplicity isn't emptiness—
it's presence without distraction.

The Weight We Put on Time

We tell ourselves
we don't have enough of it.
That it's slipping away.
That we're behind.

Still, time is not the enemy.
It's the mind's relationship to time
that creates pressure.

Always measuring.
Always comparing.
Always rushing.

Life doesn't follow the clock.
It follows the breath.
The body.
The now.

You're not behind.
You're just not here yet.

The Gift of Unrushed Attention

There's a kind of presence
that can't be rushed.

It listens fully.
It sees deeply.
It moves without hurry.

To give something your full attention
is to make it sacred.

Not because it changes—
but because you do.

In that pause,
you remember how to truly be with life.

No multitasking.
No effort to move on.

Just this.
Just now.
Just one thing fully.

Slowness Reveals More

The slower you go,
the more you see.

Subtle textures.
Unspoken feelings.
The space between things.

Slowness opens your perception.
It sharpens your senses.
It deepens your presence.

Most of what matters in life
is missed in a hurry.

The sacred isn't louder—
it's quieter.

You don't need more time.
You need more presence in the time you have.

Listening to the Quiet

There is a quiet
beneath the noise.

Not the absence of sound,
but the presence of stillness.

It doesn't shout.
It doesn't interrupt.
It waits.

And when you slow down enough,
you begin to hear it.

The soft rhythm of breath.
The silence behind every sound.
The gentle pulse of now.

The quiet has always been speaking—
you were just listening to something else.

Slow Down.

Everything Real Is Here.

CHAPTER 4

BEYOND
THOUGHT,
INTO
AWARENESS

You Are Not Your Thoughts

Thoughts arise—

sometimes helpful,

sometimes hurtful,

sometimes random.

But they are not you.

They come and go,

just like clouds in a wide sky.

You are not the cloud.

You are the sky.

You are the space they move through.

The awareness that sees them.

No thought can define you.

No thought can contain what you are.

You are not what appears in awareness—

you are the awareness itself.

The Mind's Habit of Grasping

The mind wants to hold on.

To understand.

To label.

To control.

It grasps at meaning,

grasps at identity,

grasps at permanence—

in a world that offers none.

But grasping creates tension.

And tension blocks clarity.

The tighter the mind holds,

the less you see.

When you let go of the need to grasp,

something opens.

Awareness doesn't grasp—

it simply sees.

The Space Between Thoughts

Thoughts come and go.
And between them—
there is space.

A soft, open silence.
Unnoticed, yet always there.

You don't have to silence the mind.
You only have to notice
what surrounds it.

That space is not empty.
It's alive.
Still.
Aware.

You are not the thought that speaks.
You are the silence that listens.

The space between thoughts
is not a gap.
It's who you are.

You Are Not the Thought.

You Are Here Before It.

Awareness Doesn't Argue

The mind wants to be right.
It wants to prove, defend, define.

But awareness doesn't argue.
It doesn't choose sides.
It doesn't take offense.

It simply sees.

Thoughts rise and fall
like waves on the surface—
but awareness remains still beneath them.

There's no need to win.
No need to explain.

Truth doesn't shout.
It rests in what sees all things clearly.

Letting Thoughts Come and Go

You don't have to chase every thought.
You don't have to push them away either.

Let them arise.
Let them pass.
Like clouds through an open sky.

Awareness doesn't cling.
It doesn't resist.

It simply watches.

You're not here to control the weather.
You're here to remember
that the sky was never touched by the storm.

Peace doesn't come from stopping thoughts—
it comes from not following them.

Who You Are Is Always Here

Thoughts change.

Emotions shift.

Circumstances rise and fall.

Still, something in you

remains.

The awareness that sees.

The stillness that stays.

You are not what moves.

You are what witnesses movement.

Not the waves,

but the ocean beneath.

Not the storm,

but the sky that holds it.

What you are

is not an experience—

it is the one who experiences.

A Thought is Not the Truth

Just because a thought appears
doesn't make it true.

The mind will say many things—
about who you are,
what you're worth,
what will or won't happen.

But thought is not truth.
It's interpretation.
It's habit.
It's noise.

Awareness doesn't argue with thought.
It simply sees through it.

You don't have to believe everything you think.
You only have to notice
that you're thinking.

The Quiet That Holds Everything

There is a quiet
beneath the mind.

Not the silence of nothing—
but the silence of everything.

It holds thought,
but is not thought.
It holds emotion,
but is not emotion.

This quiet is not something you reach.
It's what remains
when you stop searching.

It doesn't need fixing.
It doesn't need words.

It's the space that lets everything be—
and is changed by nothing at all.

Thoughts Pass.

Awareness Remains.

CHAPTER 5

THE POWER

OF

SURRENDER

Resistance is What Hurts

It's not the moment itself
that creates the pain.

It's the resistance to the moment.

The pushing.
The tightening.
The refusal to let things be as they are.

We think we're protecting ourselves.
Yet resistance only adds weight.

The moment isn't always easy.
But it becomes harder
when we fight it.

It's not life that hurts—
it's how tightly we hold it.

What Surrender Really Means

Surrender isn't giving up.
It's giving over.

Not to defeat,
but to reality.

It's the quiet strength
of no longer resisting what already is.

Surrender doesn't mean
you stop caring.

It means you stop controlling
what was never yours to control.

There is power in letting go—
not because you lose,
but because you finally rest.

Surrender is not weakness.
It's trust in motion.

Acceptance is Not Agreement

Acceptance doesn't mean
you approve of everything.

It doesn't mean
you condone pain,
or celebrate loss,
or stay silent in the face of harm.

Acceptance means
you stop denying what already is.

You stop arguing with the moment.

Only from there
can real change begin.
Only from there
can peace enter.

Acceptance is not passive—
it's the ground where clarity begins.

Let Go.

You Are Already Held.

Letting Life Move Through You

You are not separate
from the movement of life.

You are not standing outside it,
trying to steer it.

You are part of the flow.
Held by it.
Moved by it.

When you stop trying to shape everything,
you begin to feel
what wants to move through you.

Emotion.
Insight.
Stillness.
Love.

Letting go isn't giving up—
it's allowing what's true to come alive.

Trusting What You Cannot See

Not everything real
can be seen.

There is a rhythm beneath things.
A quiet intelligence
moving even when you feel lost.

The mind wants a reason.
It wants a map.
It wants certainty.

But the heart knows how to move
without needing to see the whole path.

What's unfolding may not make sense yet.
Even so, that doesn't mean it isn't sacred.

Not all guidance is loud.
Some of it is silence
asking you to trust.

The Peace of Letting Go

Letting go isn't always easy.

Sometimes it feels like loss.

Sometimes it feels like free fall.

But beneath the fear,

there is space.

There is stillness.

There is peace.

Letting go doesn't leave you empty—

it makes room.

Room for clarity.

Room for grace.

Room for something new.

You don't find peace

by holding on.

You find it

by releasing the need to hold.

Saying Yes to the Moment

Saying yes doesn't mean
you enjoy every moment.

It means you stop resisting it.
You meet it fully,
without turning away.

Even in discomfort,
there is something to receive.

Even in challenge,
there is something to open to.

Saying yes isn't agreement—
it's presence.

It's the willingness
to stand inside your life
instead of outside of it.

Every time you say yes
to what's here,
you return to what's real.

Let It Be Enough

This moment may not be perfect.
It may not look how you hoped.

But it's here.
It's real.
It's alive.

And it's already enough.

Not because it fulfills every desire—
but because it's what's true.

When you stop measuring the moment
against what it could have been,
you start to feel the peace
of what it is.

Life doesn't need to be different
to be sacred.
It only needs to be seen.

This Moment Is Enough.

Let It Be.

CHAPTER 6

THE STILLNESS
BENEATH
IT ALL

Beneath the Noise

Life is full of sound.

Motion.

Momentum.

The mind races.

The world pulls.

Everything feels loud.

But beneath it all—

there is stillness.

A presence untouched

by movement or noise.

It doesn't need to be created.

It's already here,

beneath the doing,

beneath the thoughts,

beneath the world.

Stillness isn't found by adding.

It's found by noticing

what never left.

Nature Knows Stillness

Stillness isn't just silence—
it's presence without strain.

You see it in the way
a tree stands.
A mountain rests.
A river flows
without rushing itself.

Nature isn't in a hurry.
It doesn't try to be anything
other than what it is.

It breathes,
it opens,
it moves when it's time.

Stillness isn't something to achieve—
it's something to remember
through the simplicity of being.

The Stillness Within

There is a stillness
inside you, too.

It's not an escape.
It's not a withdrawal.

It's the space
beneath reaction.
Beneath fear.
Beneath thought.

You don't have to go anywhere to find it.
You only have to stop leaving it.

It's here
when you're quiet.
When you're listening.
When you're simply being.

You are not separate from stillness—
you are made of it.

You Don't Reach Stillness.

You Return to It.

Silence is Not Empty

Silence can feel strange at first.

Unfamiliar.

Uncomfortable.

And yet, it isn't empty.

It's full—

of presence,

of awareness,

of everything the noise was covering.

Silence isn't a void.

It's an invitation.

To feel.

To notice.

To return.

The more you soften into silence,

the more you realize—

it's not absence.

It's home.

Letting the Mind Settle

You don't need to fight the mind.
You don't need to silence it.

Just stop feeding it.
Let it slow.
Let it settle.

Like stirred water returning to clarity.
It doesn't happen through force.
It happens through stillness.

The more space you give it,
the more it rests.

Thoughts may come,
but they don't stay.
And neither do you.

You return
to the stillness that holds it all.

Being Held by the Moment

You don't have to hold the moment.
It's already holding you.

There's nothing to manage.
Nothing to force.

You can soften.
You can release.
You can be.

When you stop trying to carry it all,
you begin to feel what's always been carrying
you.

Not the mind.
Not the effort.
But the deeper rhythm
beneath everything.

Stillness is not something you hold—
it's what holds you.

Beneath Everything,

You Are Already at Rest.

CHAPTER 7

THE SIMPLICITY

OF

BEING

Nothing to Prove

The mind wants to earn everything.

To justify its worth.

To prove it belongs.

But being doesn't require proof.

You are here.

You are aware.

You exist.

That's enough.

You don't need to impress the moment.

You don't need to outperform your presence.

The more you let go of needing to become,

the more you remember

you already are.

You are not here to prove.

You are here to be.

The Effortless Nature of Presence

You don't have to try to be present.
Presence is already here.

The effort comes from the mind—
trying to grasp,
to focus,
to control the now.

Awareness, however, doesn't try.
It just is.

The more you relax,
the more you notice
it's never been missing.

You don't become present.
You notice that you are.

Presence is not created—
it's uncovered.

Being is Enough

You don't need to do more
to be worthy of this moment.

You don't need to fix yourself
to deserve peace.

Being is not a task.
It's not a role.
It's not a performance.

It's the simple truth
beneath all doing—
you exist.

And in that,
you are already whole.

You don't need to earn this breath.
You only need to receive it.

There Is Nothing To Prove.

You Already Are.

Let Life Be Simple

You don't need to manage every moment.

You don't have to shape every outcome.

You don't need a plan for how everything will unfold.

Life has its own rhythm.

Its own way of working things out.

You're allowed to pause.

To do less.

To simply be with what's here.

The more you let go of the need to control,

the more you begin to feel

how naturally things move without effort.

Simplicity is not passive—

it's trust in motion.

The Beauty of Doing Nothing

We've been taught
to equate stillness with laziness,
rest with waste.

But presence isn't unproductive.
It's alive.
It's whole.

There is a beauty
in doing nothing.

Not out of avoidance—
but out of peace.

When you stop needing every moment
to be filled or fixed,
you begin to feel
what it truly means to be.

Sometimes the most important thing
is to do nothing at all.

The Grace of Simplicity

Simplicity is not lack.

It's clarity.

It's space.

It's peace without the clutter.

The more present you become,

the less you need.

Not because you're deprived—

but because you're full.

You start to see beauty

in the quiet things.

The ordinary things.

The things that don't shout to be seen.

Simplicity isn't less.

It's the fullness of what remains

when nothing is in the way.

The Quiet Gift of Being Here

You don't need a reason
to feel grateful.

Sometimes it arises
without effort—
when you slow down
and really see what's around you.

The curve of a branch.
The warmth of light.
The breath that arrives on its own.

Gratitude is not something you chase.
It's what blooms
when presence is enough.

Wholeness Has No Requirements

You don't become whole
by achieving.

You don't earn it
by effort,
by improvement,
by proving your worth.

Wholeness isn't a reward.
It's your natural state.

Even when you're tired.
Even when the mind is busy.
Even when you forget.

Nothing can add to what you already are—
and nothing can take it away.

Peace Is Found Where

Nothing Extra Is Needed.

CHAPTER 8

LIVE

FULLY

PRESENT

Life is Happening Now

This is it.

Not the future you imagined.

Not the moment you're waiting for.

This breath.

This heartbeat.

This now.

We miss it looking forward.

We miss it looking back.

But life never moved.

Only our attention did.

To live fully present

is not to escape life—

it's to finally meet it.

There is no better moment than this one.

There never was.

Presence is the Practice

There's nothing more to wait for.
No perfect day.
No ideal version of you.

This moment is enough to begin.

Not by changing it—
but by showing up to it.

Presence isn't a destination.
It's a way of being
that meets life exactly as it is.

And the more you return,
the more natural it becomes.

Not because life gets easier—
but because you are finally here for it.

The Presence in Everyday Things

Presence doesn't just live in deep conversations
or mountaintop moments.

It lives in the way you wash a dish.
The way you tie your shoes.
The way you greet the morning light.

It lives in breath.
In attention.
In the pause before speaking.

When you give yourself fully
to the simple act of being here,
even the ordinary becomes sacred.

Let Life Touch You

To live fully present
is to live fully open.

To let beauty move you.
To let sorrow soften you.
To let joy rise without holding it back.

This isn't about perfection.
It's about participation.

Presence invites you to feel,
to care,
to be here without hiding.

When you stop protecting yourself from life,
you begin to feel how deeply it loves you.

Being Here Fully

Is the Most Sacred Art.

Presence is How You Love

You can't truly love
from a distracted mind.

Love needs your attention.
Your stillness.
Your openness.

When you are present with someone,
they feel it.
Not as words,
but as being seen.

To live fully present
is to love fully alive.

Presence is not just awareness—
it's how love takes form.

Nothing is Too Small for Presence

You don't need a special moment
to come alive.

This one is enough.
So is the next.
And the next.

Presence doesn't ask for performance—
it only asks for honesty.

Even the smallest action,
when done with full attention,
becomes an offering.

Life doesn't need to impress you.
It just wants to be met.

This Moment is the Miracle

We search for miracles—

something extraordinary,

something beyond the everyday.

But the miracle

is already here.

In the breath you didn't ask for.

In the light pouring through the trees.

In the quiet knowing that you exist.

Nothing more is needed.

Nothing more is missing.

This moment

is the miracle

you've been waiting for.

You Were Never Absent

Through all the searching,
the striving,
the forgetting—
something was always here.

Watching.
Listening.
Waiting without judgment.

The presence beneath it all.

You may have felt far away.
You may have gotten lost in thought,
in time,
in becoming.

But awareness never left.
Life never left.
You never truly left.

The journey ends where it began—
in the presence that's always been.

You Never Had To Arrive.

You Were Always Here.

THANK YOU FOR YOUR PRESENCE.

ACKNOWLEDGEMENT

This book emerged through many moments of stillness, surrender, and quiet listening. I am deeply grateful for the unseen guidance that carried it, and for the intelligence of life itself that reveals truth when we slow down enough to notice.

To those who walked beside me, supported me, and helped me remain grounded, thank you. Your presence shaped this offering more than you may realize.

To life, in all its forms, through silence and heartbreak, wonder and the natural world, thank you for being my greatest teacher.

And to you, holding these pages now, thank you for meeting this work with openness and care. If these words have helped you pause, soften, or remember

ABOUT THE AUTHOR

Gabriel Garcia is a writer devoted to presence, simplicity, and the quiet truth found in direct experience. His work does not aim to instruct or persuade, but to gently point toward what is already here, beneath thought, beneath effort, and beneath the impulse to become someone else.

Rooted in a lifelong inquiry into consciousness, stillness, and the nature of being, Gabriel's writing reflects a movement away from seeking and toward remembrance. Rather than offering methods or philosophies, he creates space for pause, for listening, and for a return to what has never been absent.

Through his platform, Live Fully Present, Gabriel shares reflections and offerings that support a lived relationship with awareness, not as an idea to understand, but as a reality to rest in. His work invites a slower pace, a softer attention, and a deeper trust in life as it unfolds

He lives simply, guided by presence, gratitude, and reverence for the ordinary. His words are not meant to lead, but to accompany, echoes of a truth that reveals itself when we stop reaching and allow this moment to be enough.

You Were Never Walking Toward It.

You Were Always Walking With It.